BONUS!

Pick up your FREE BONUS sweary word coloring pages!

Check out: **www.FckYeahColoring.com**

For more BONUS pages like this...

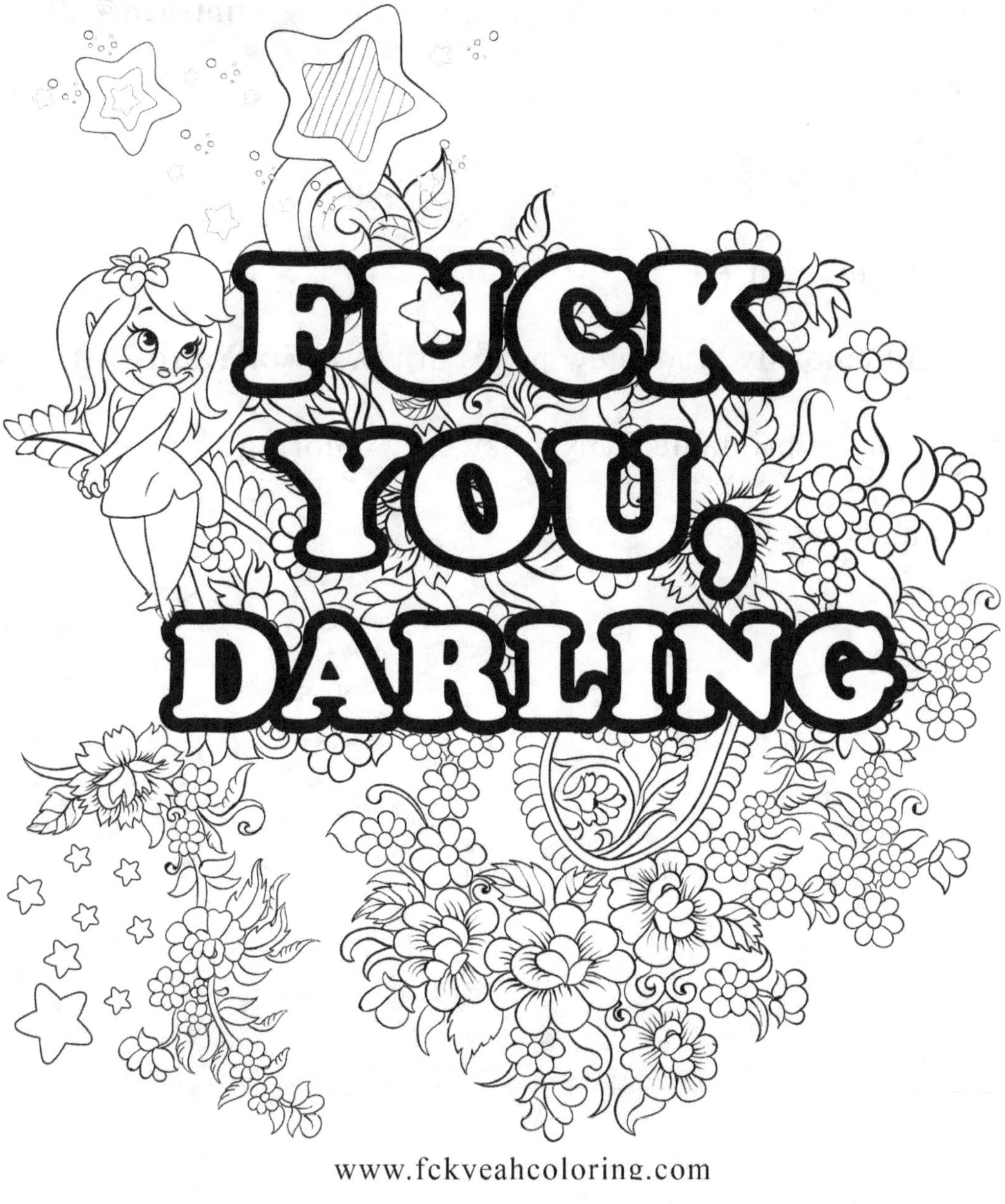

www.fckyeahcoloring.com

Dear Creative,

Have a giggle and blow off some steam!

Look through the pages, and pick out the swears that speak to you at the moment.

Just remember, these pages are 18+ and not for the faint-hearted!

I send out NEW, FREE bonus pages every couple of weeks

as a special thank you.

Grab your ridiculously crude new pages at **www.FckYeahColoring.com**

Make sure you get printable BONUS sweary coloring pages

delivered immediately!

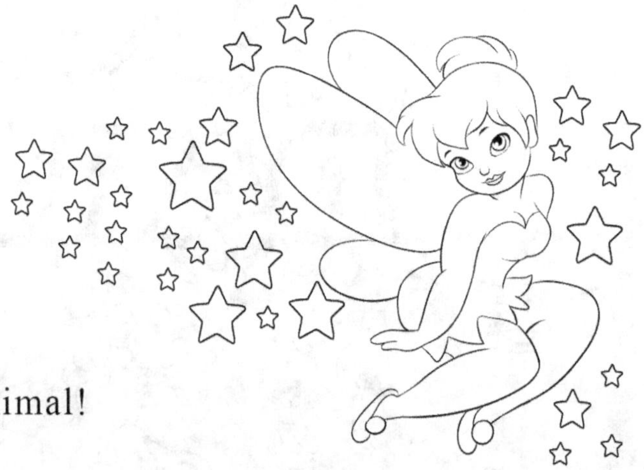

Now, enjoy coloring, you filthy animal!

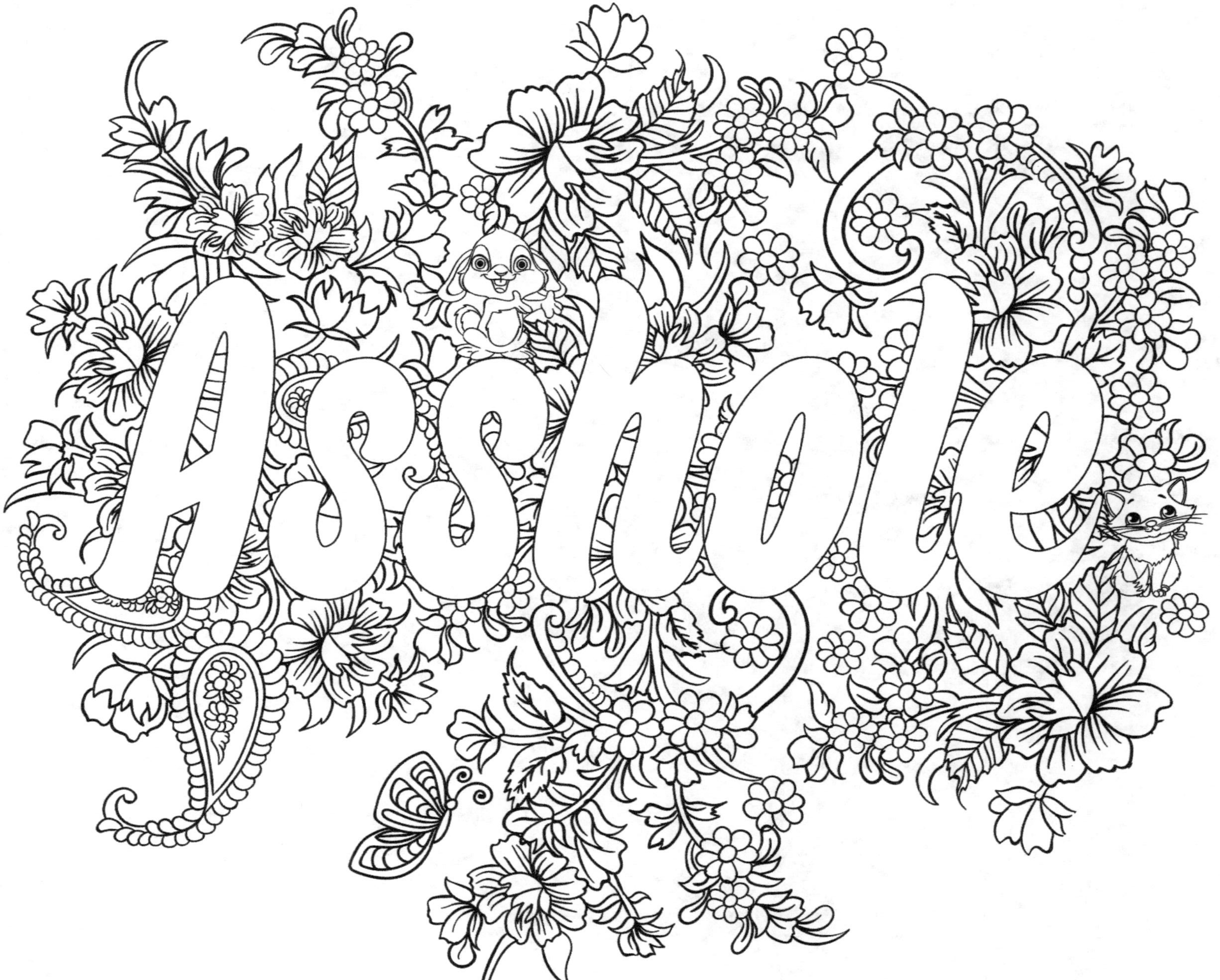
Asshole

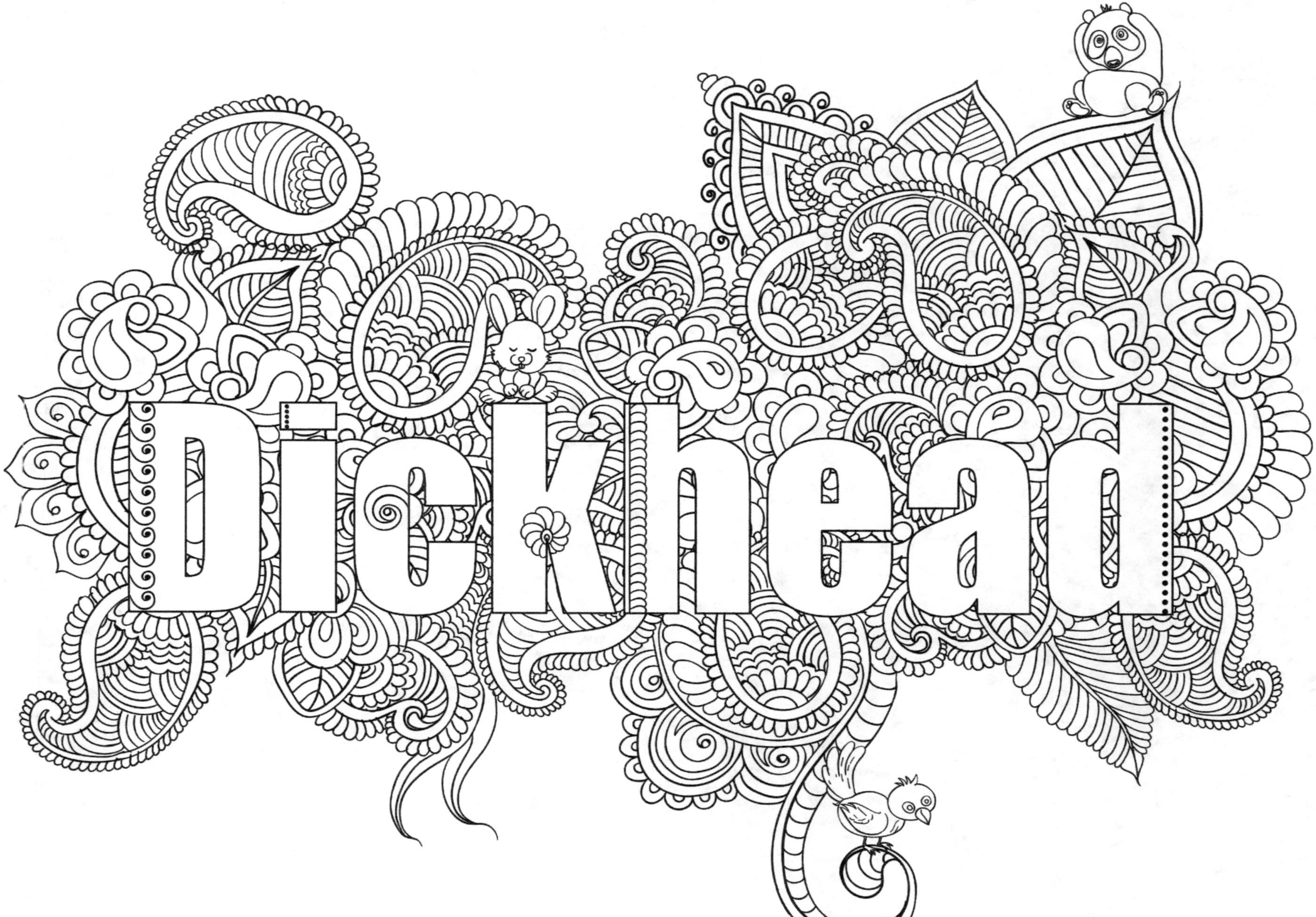
Dickhead

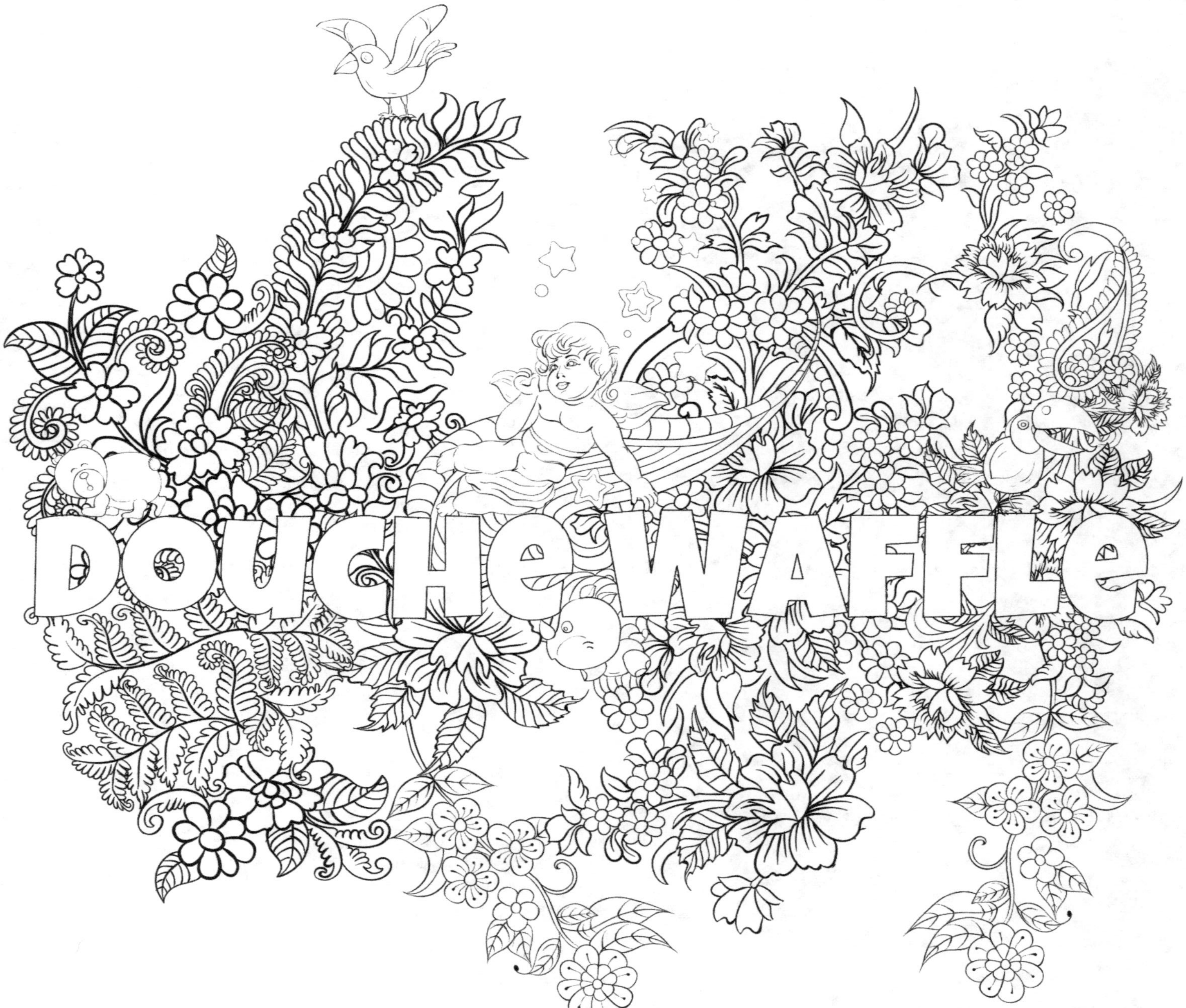
DOUCHEWAFFLE

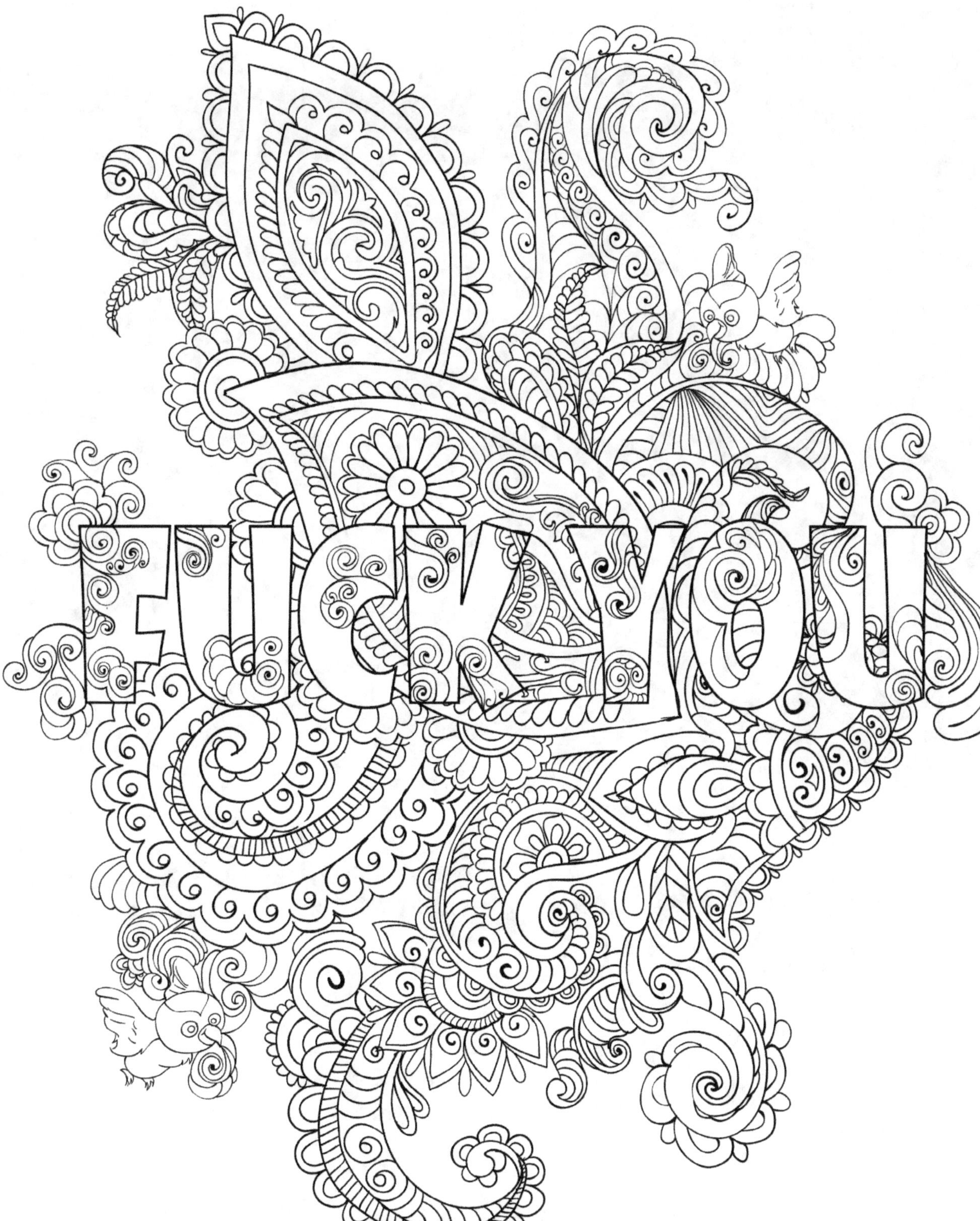
FUCK YOU

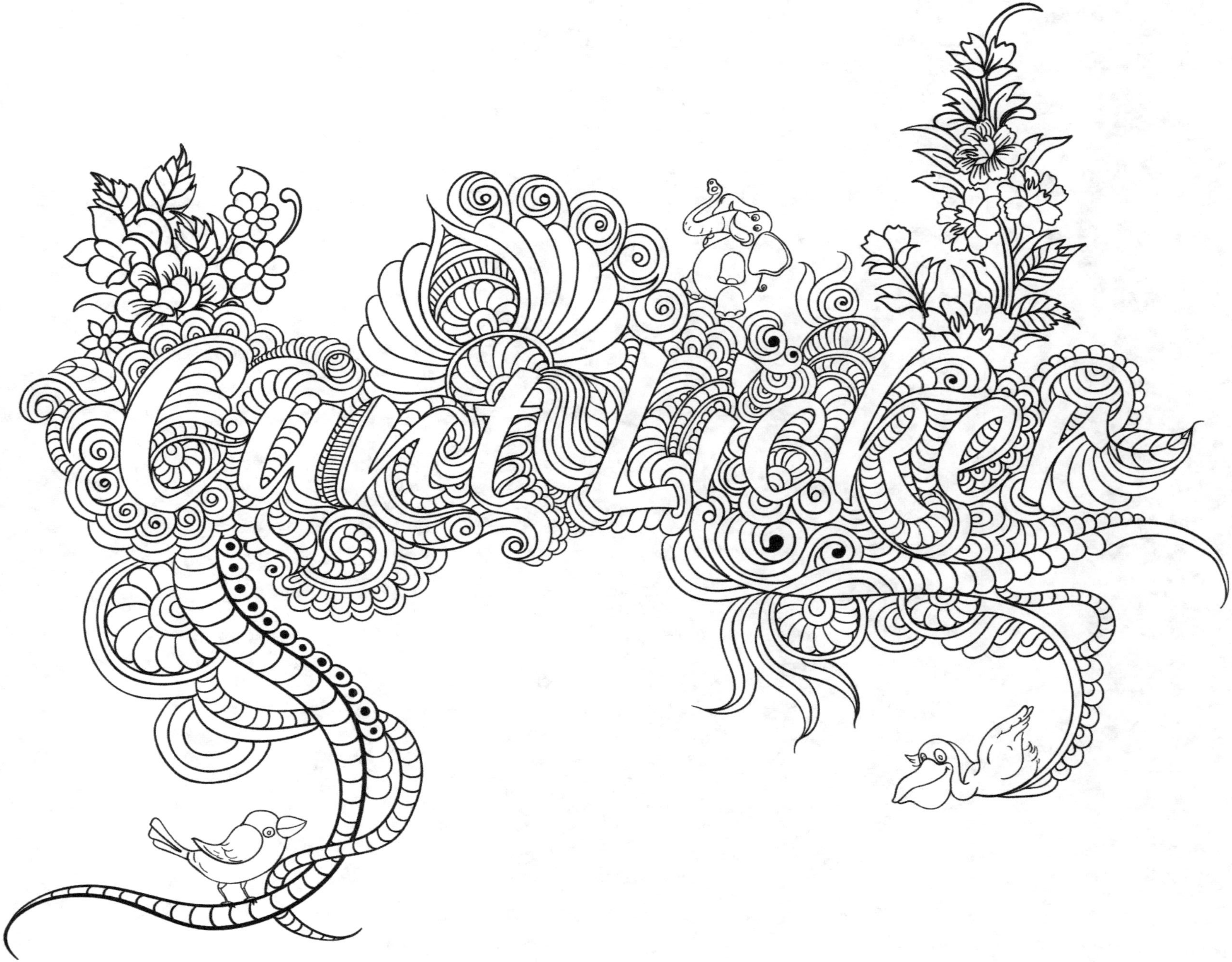
CuntLicker

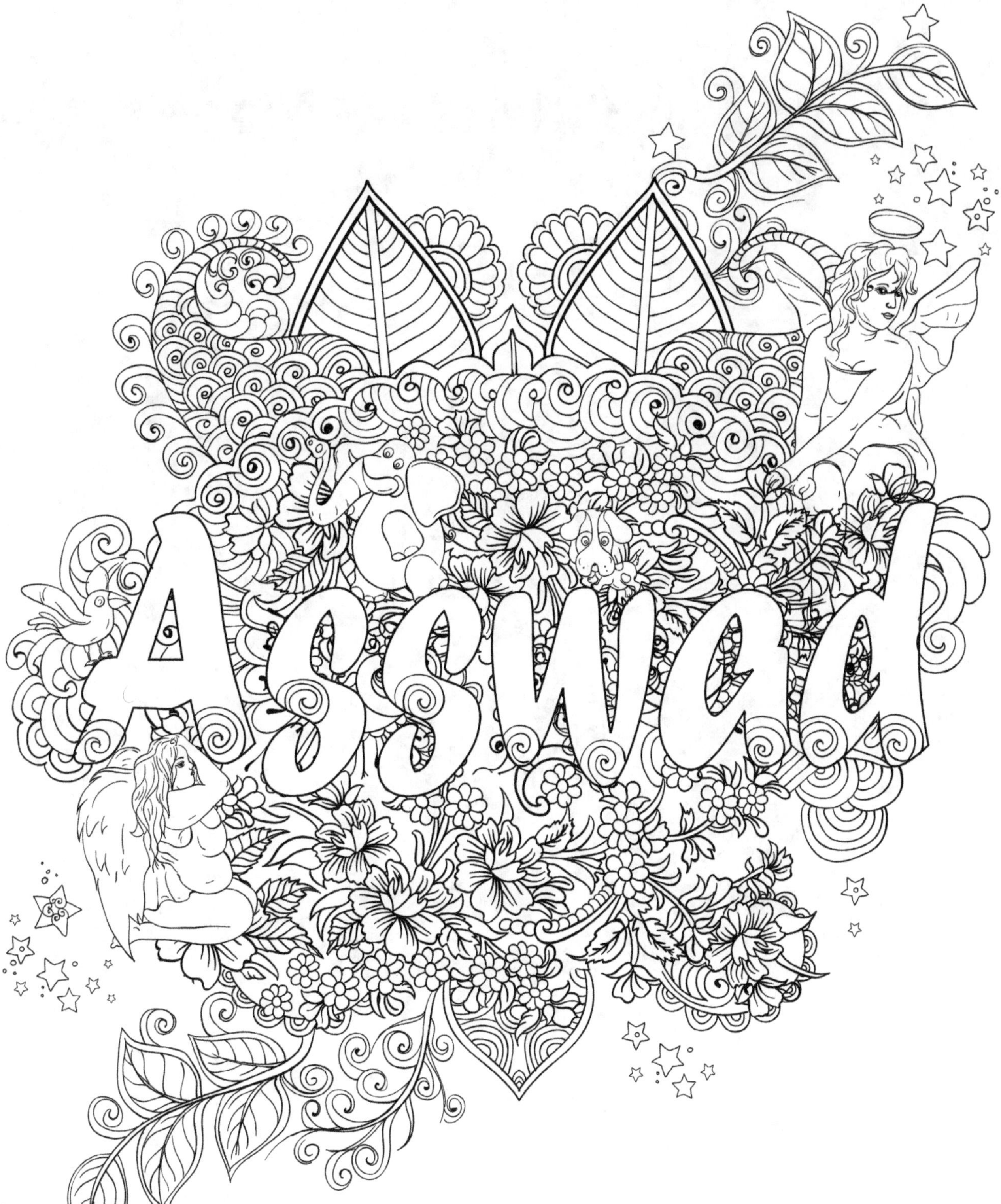
Asswad

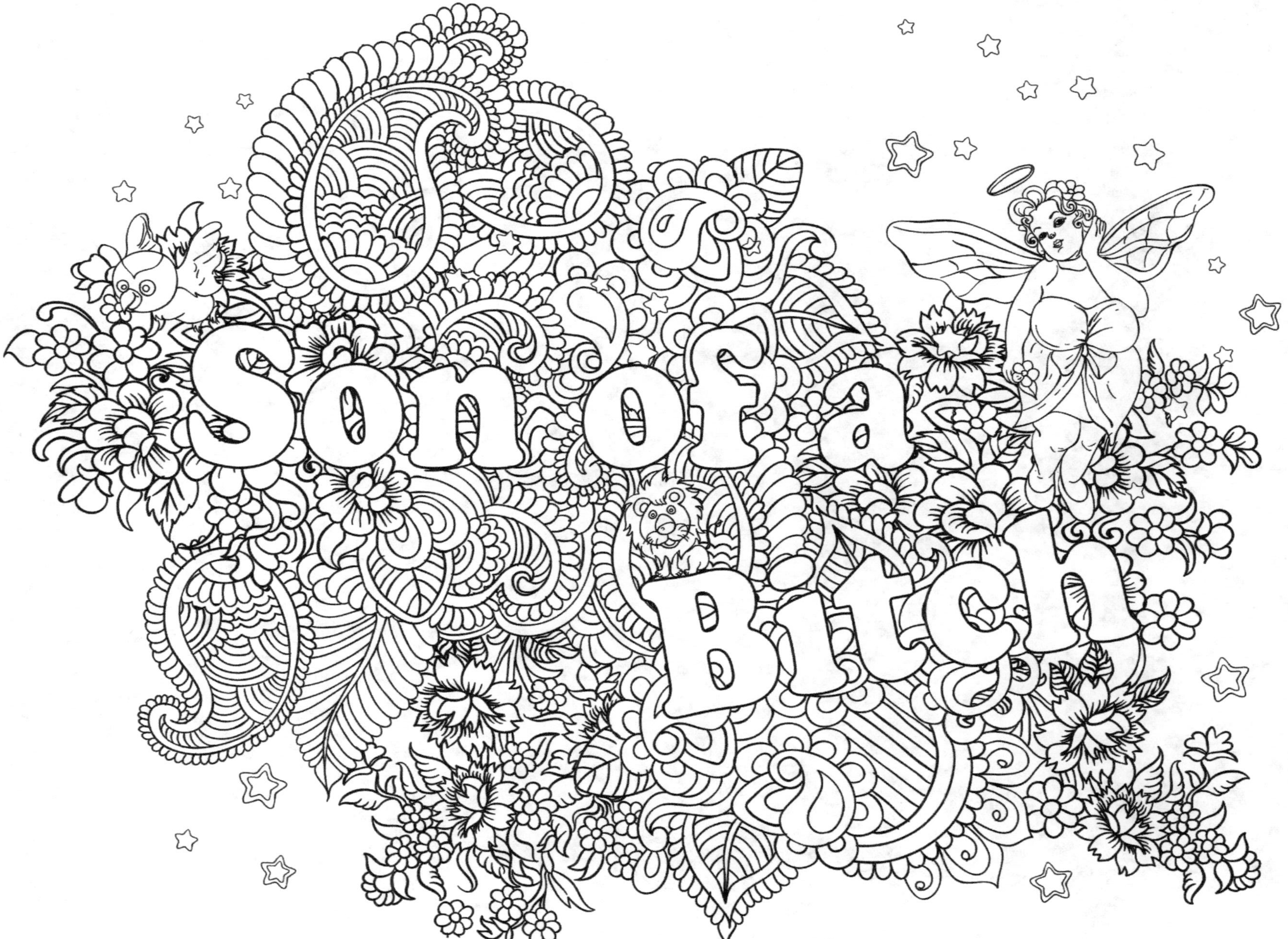
Son of a
Bitch

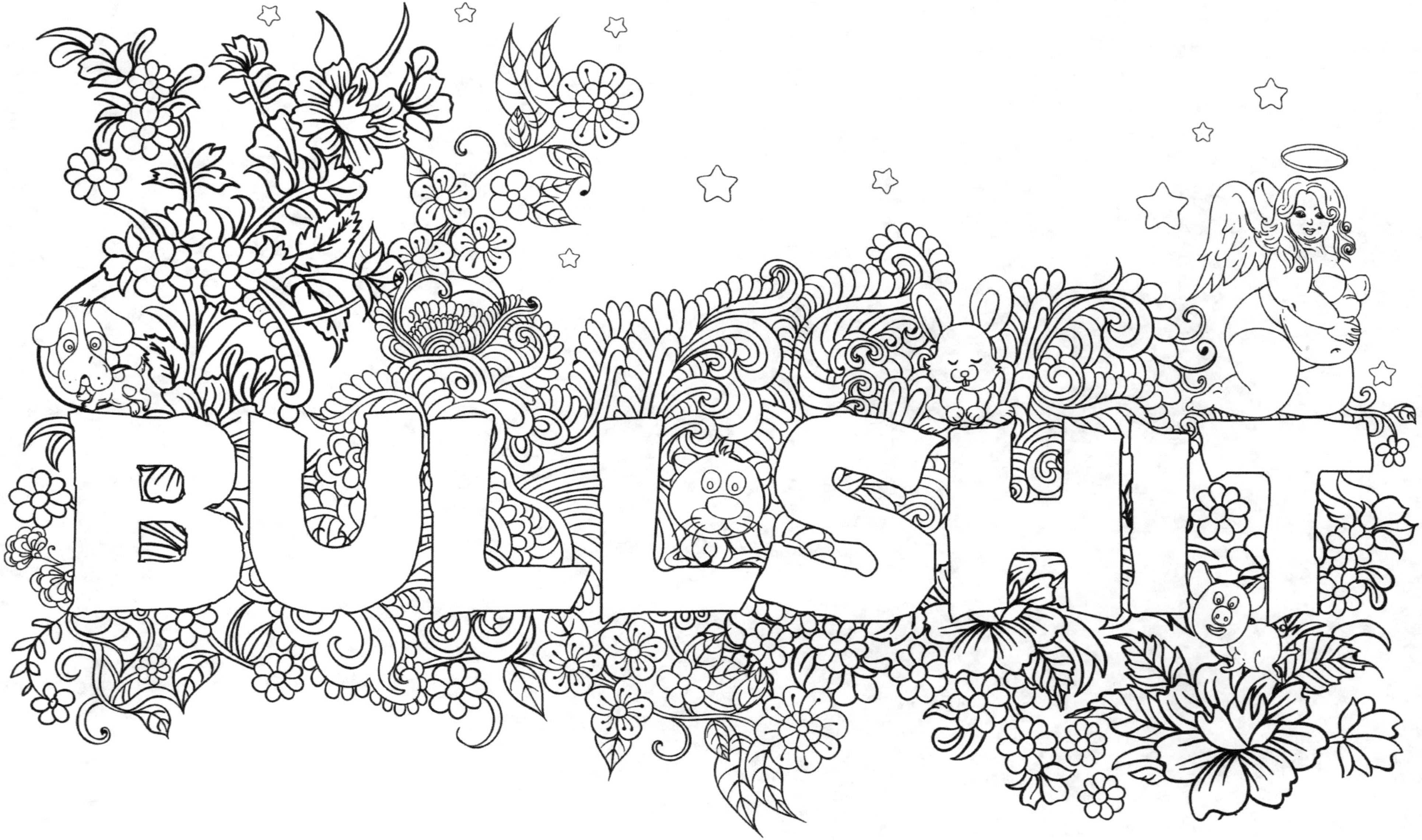
BULLSHIT

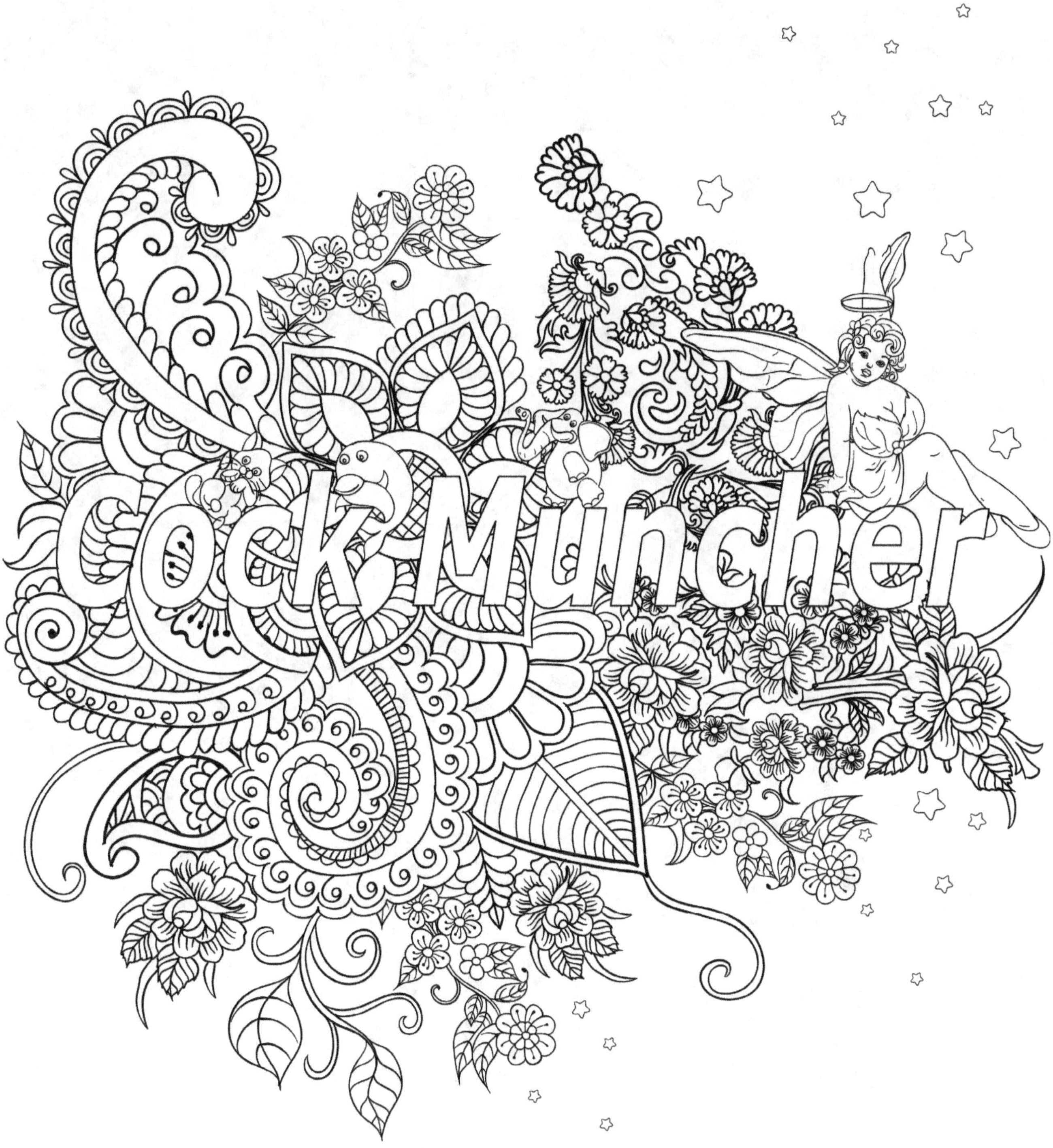
Cock Muncher

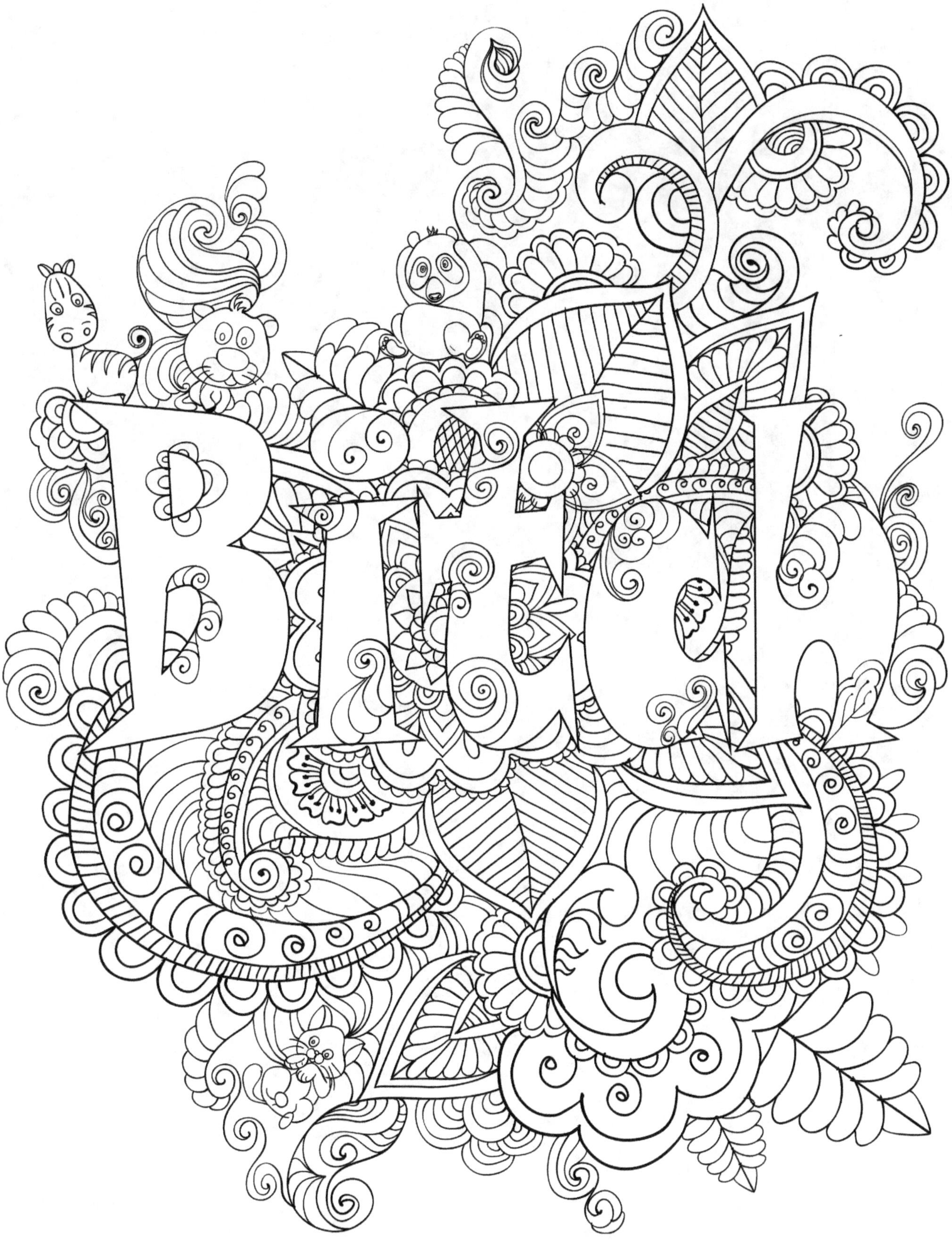
Bitch

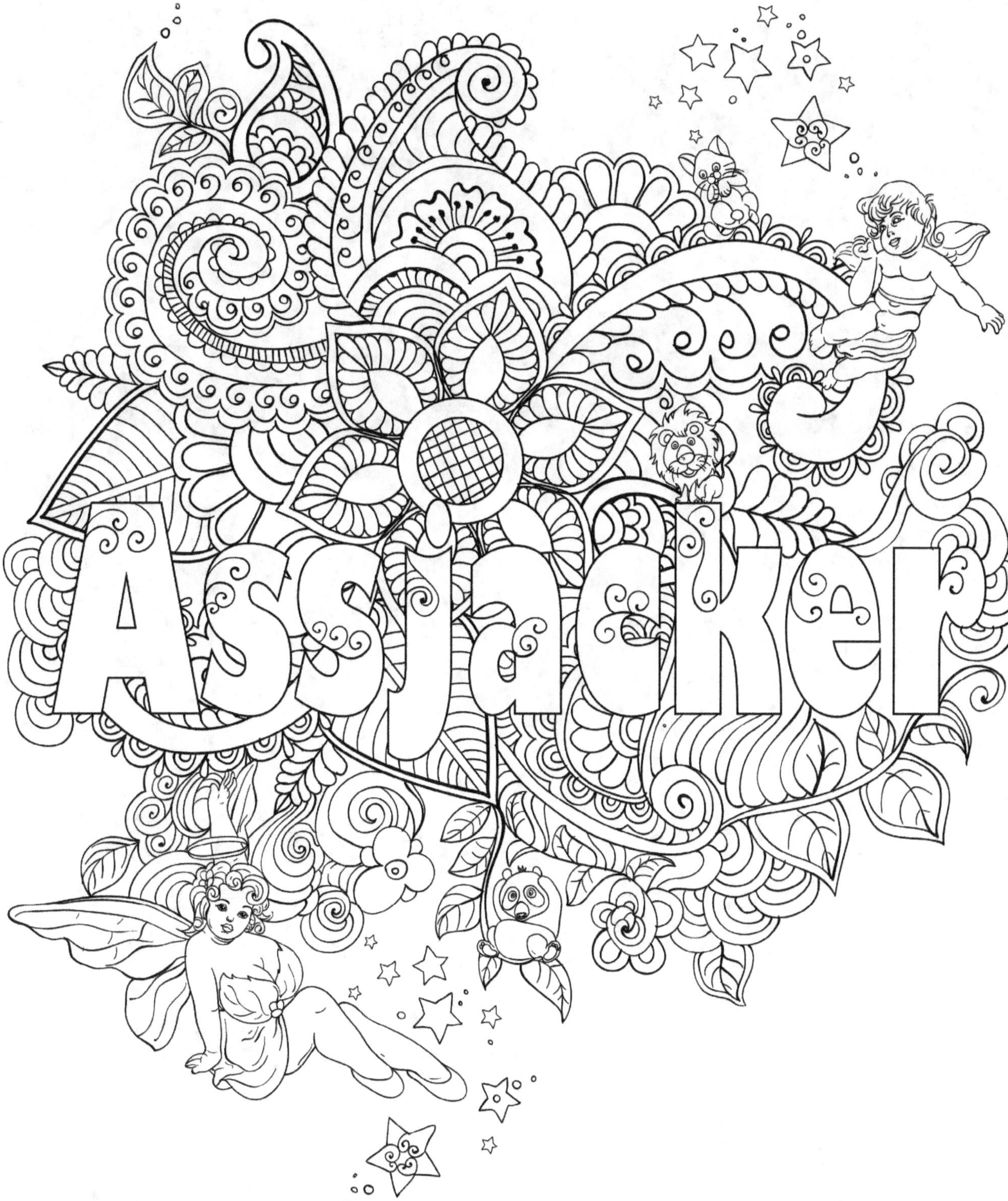
Assjacker

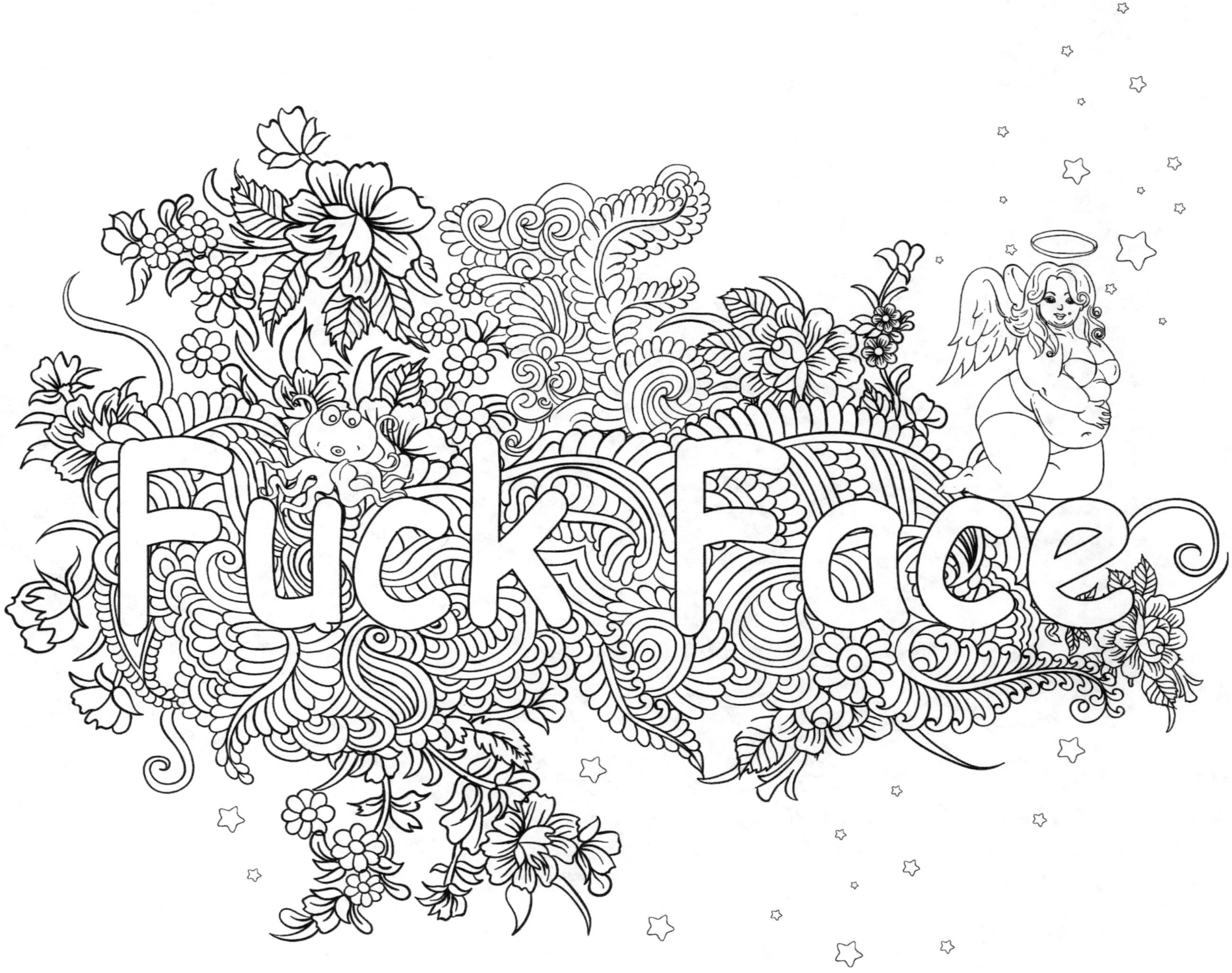
Fuck Face

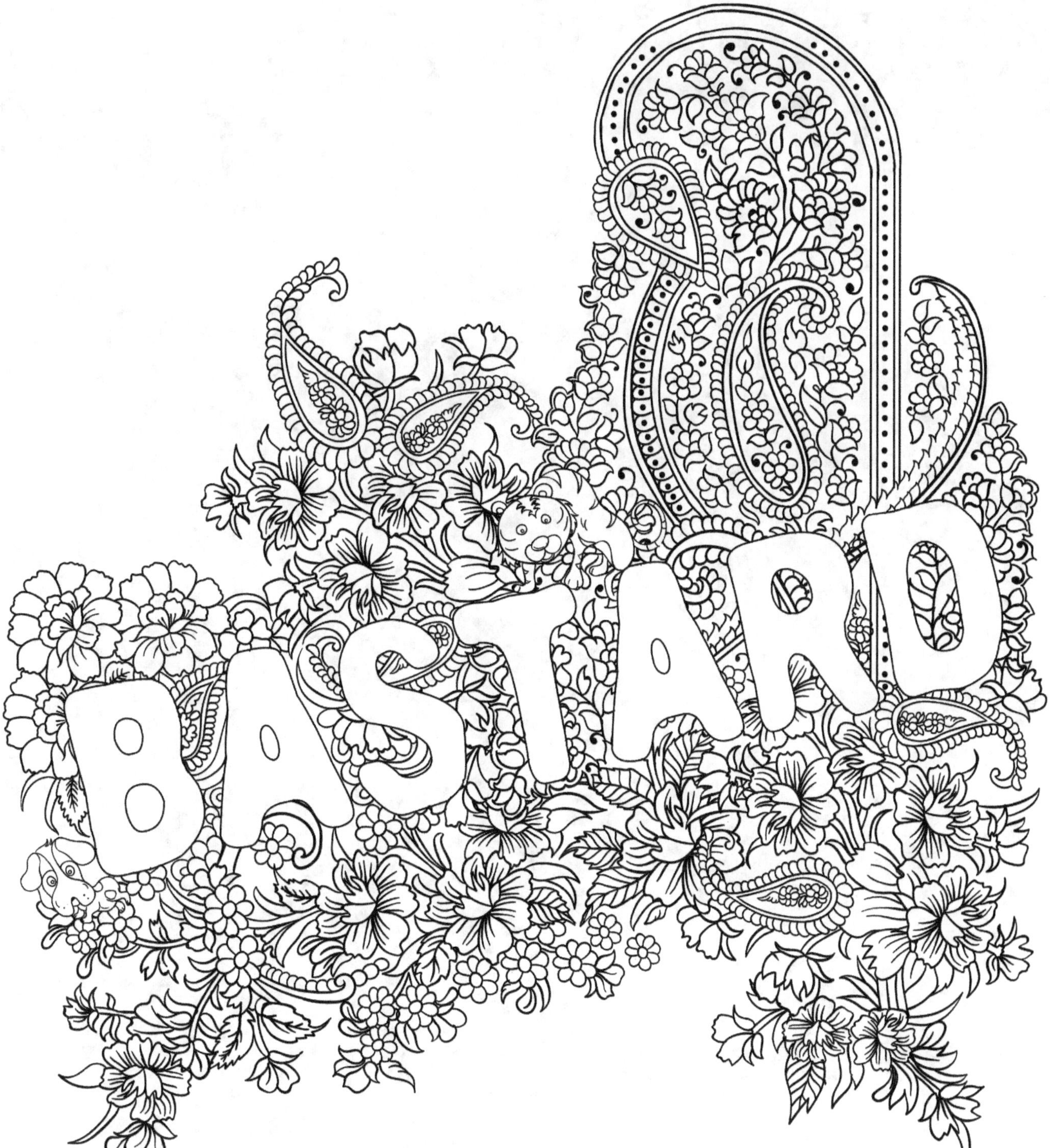
BASTARD

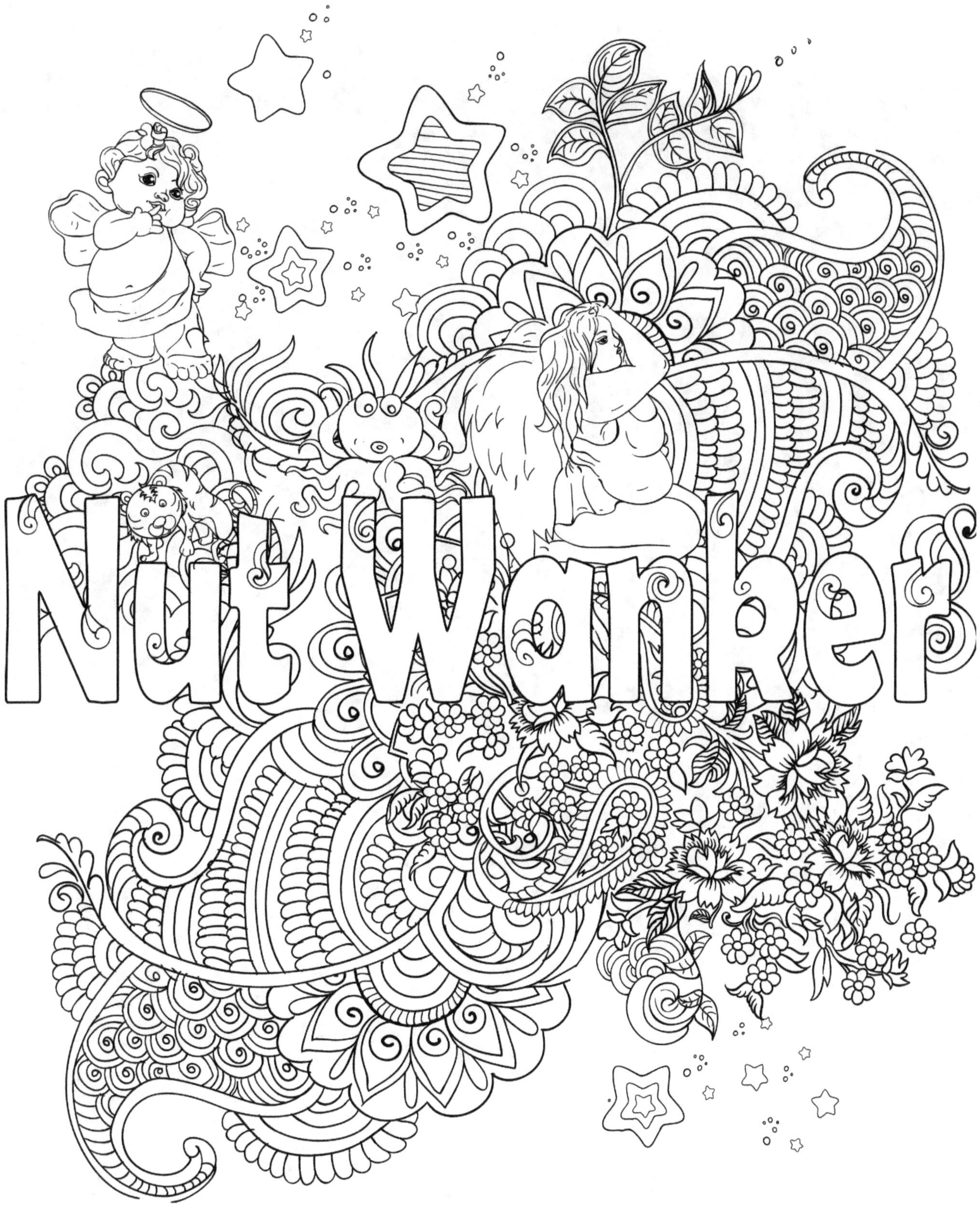
Nut Wanker

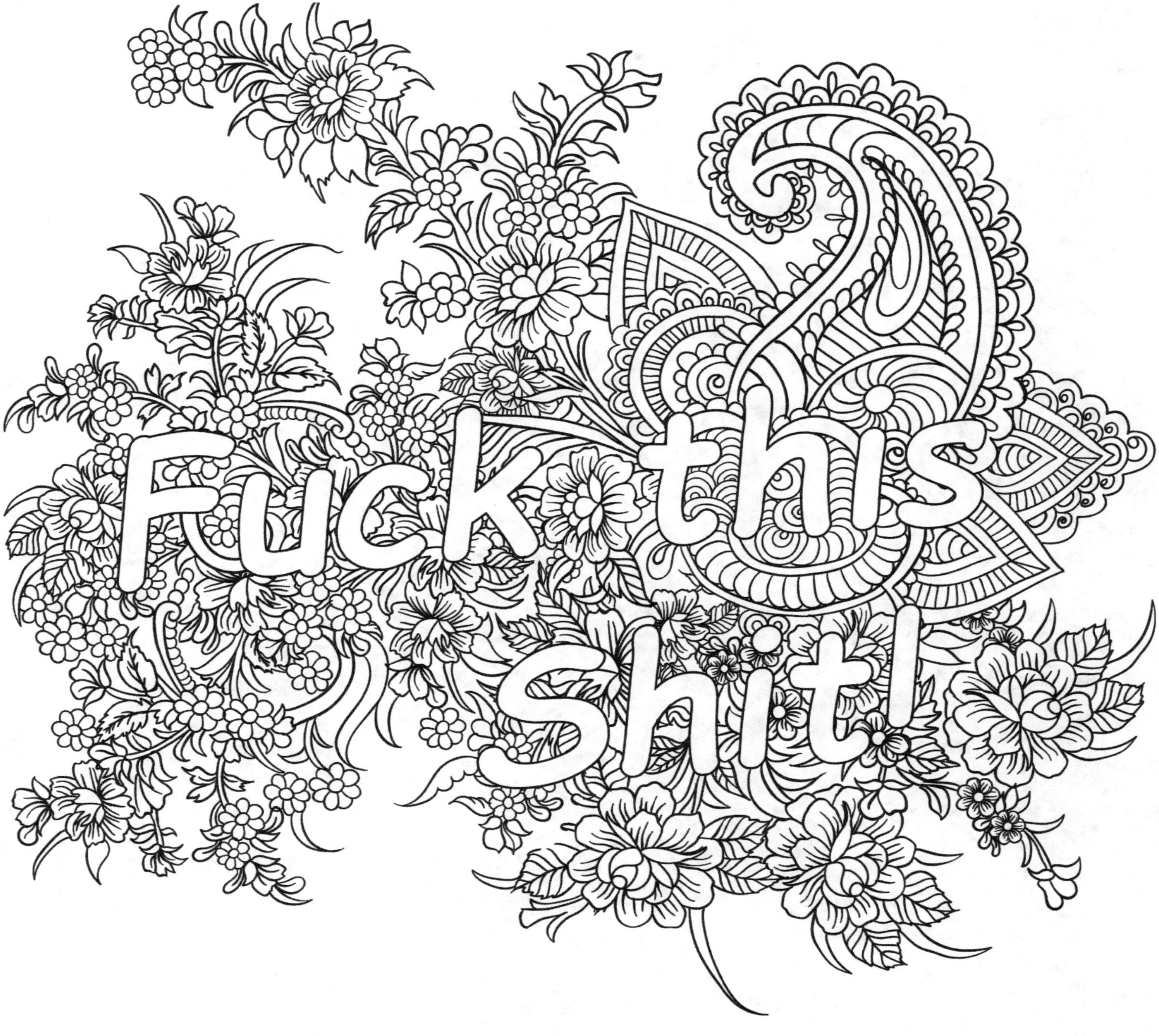
Fuck this
Shit!

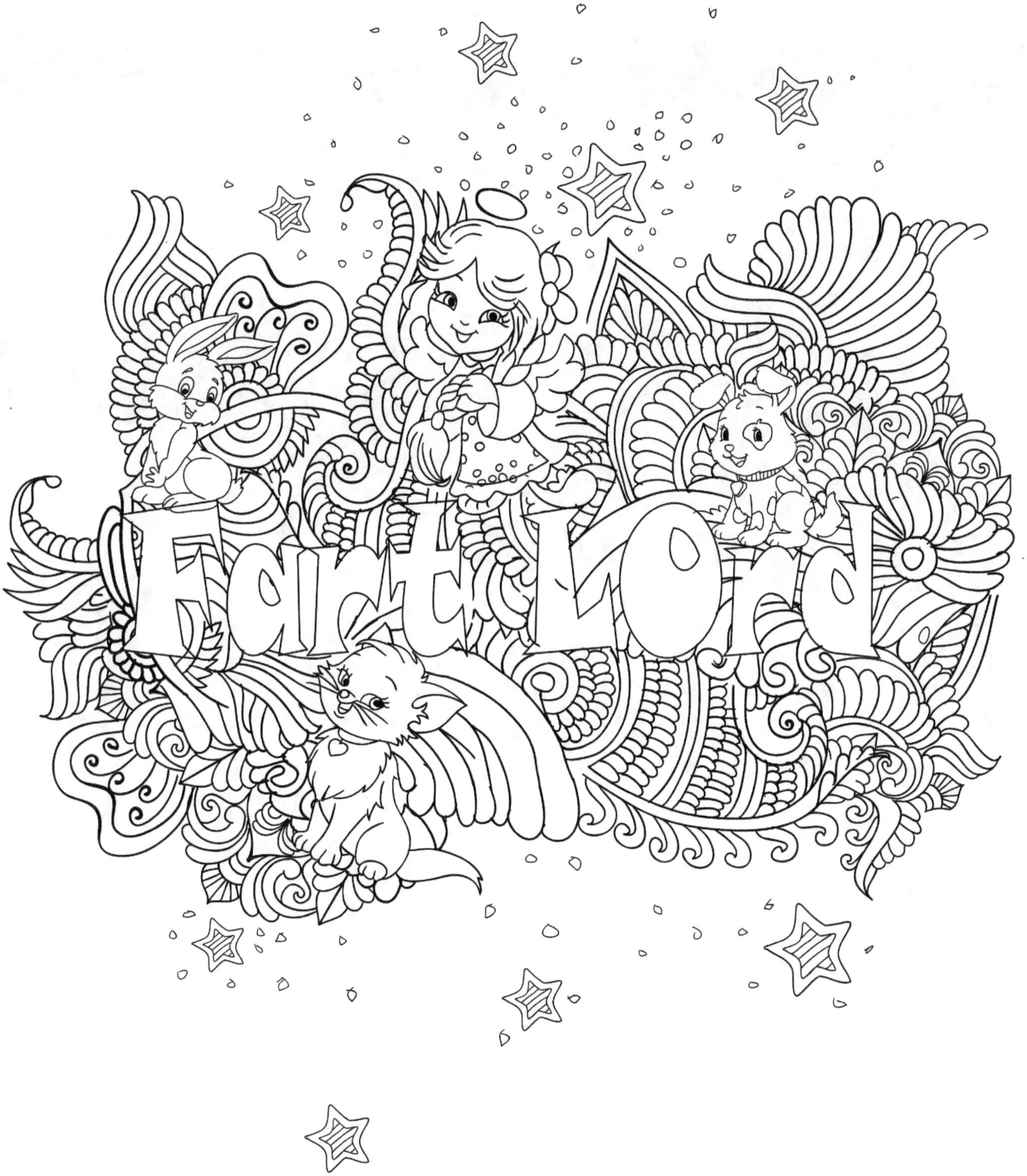
Fart Lord

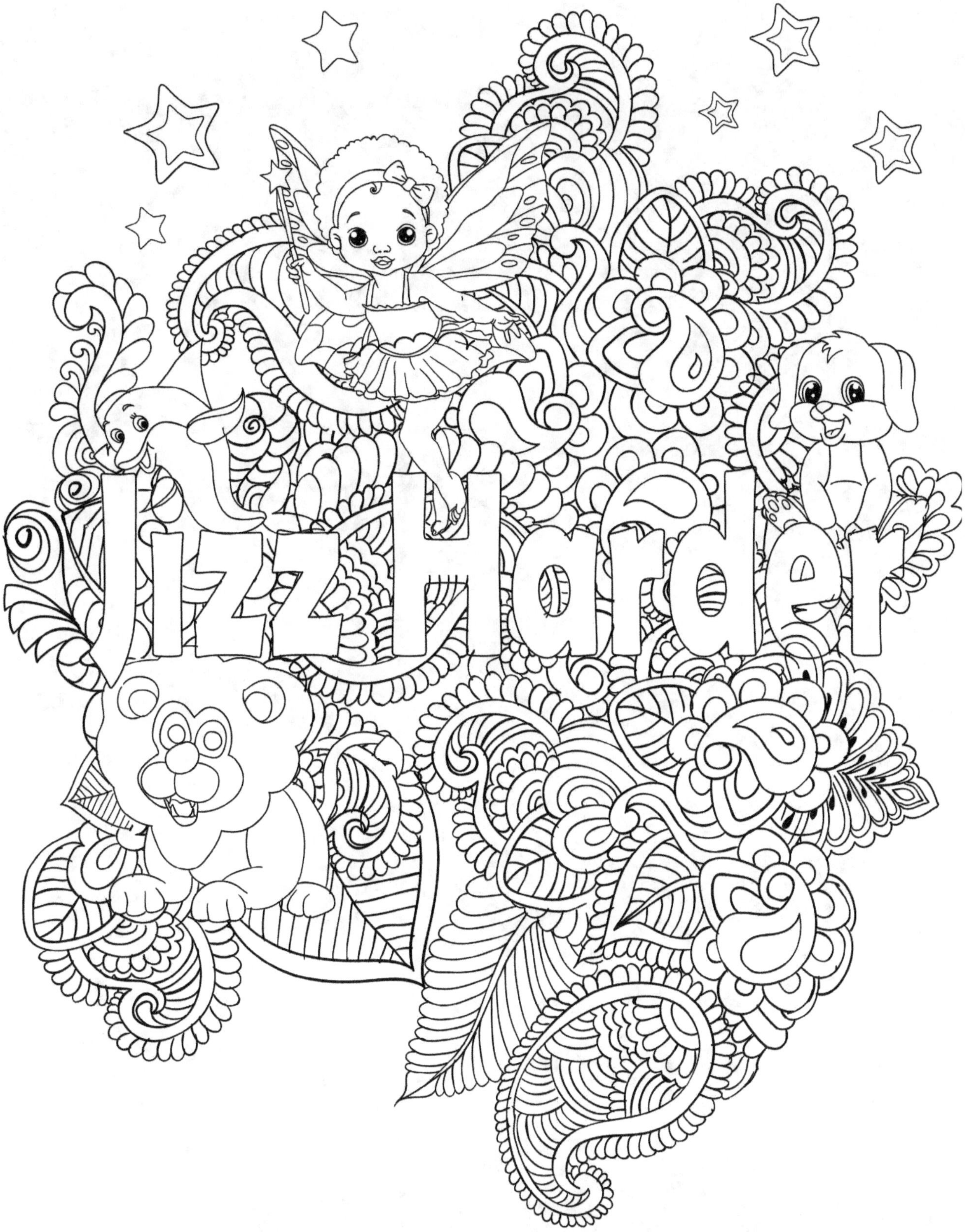
Jizz Harder

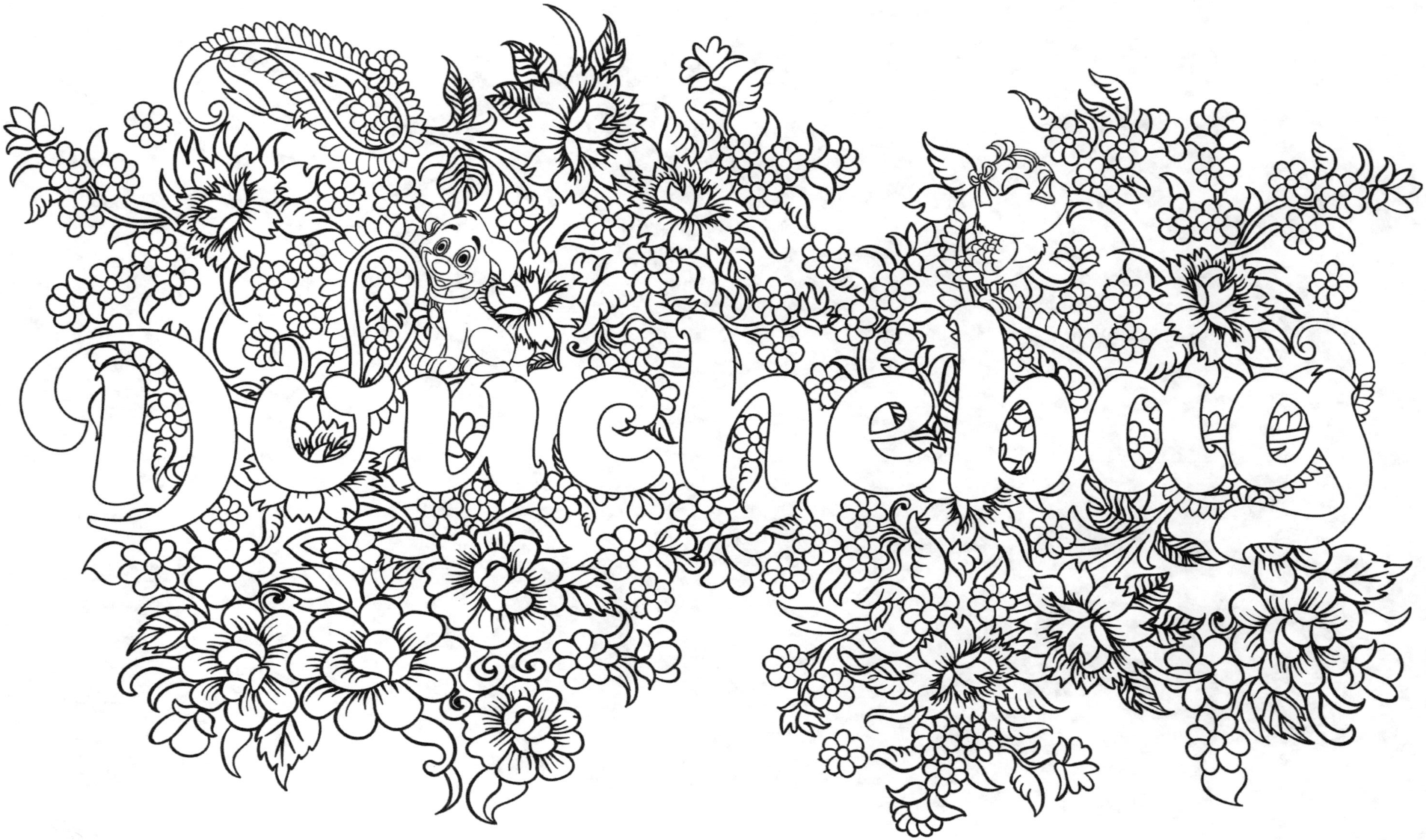
Douchebag

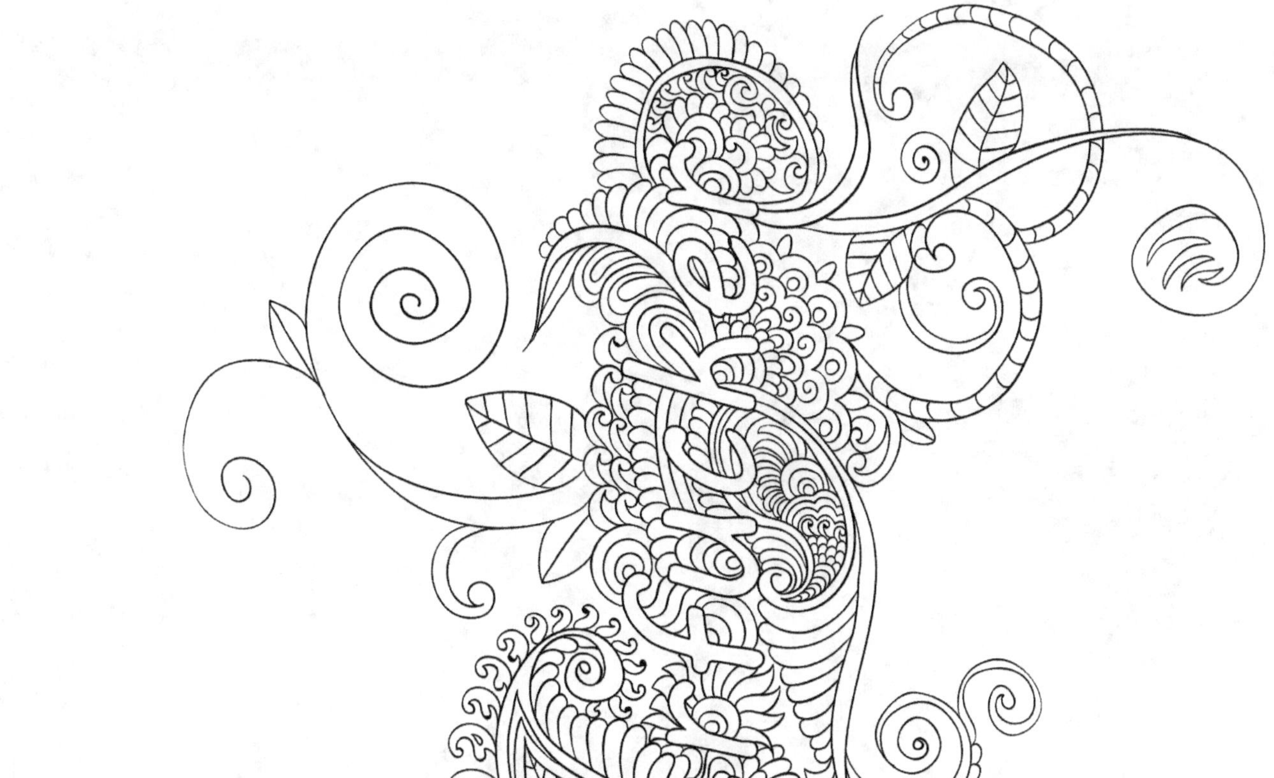
Motherfucker

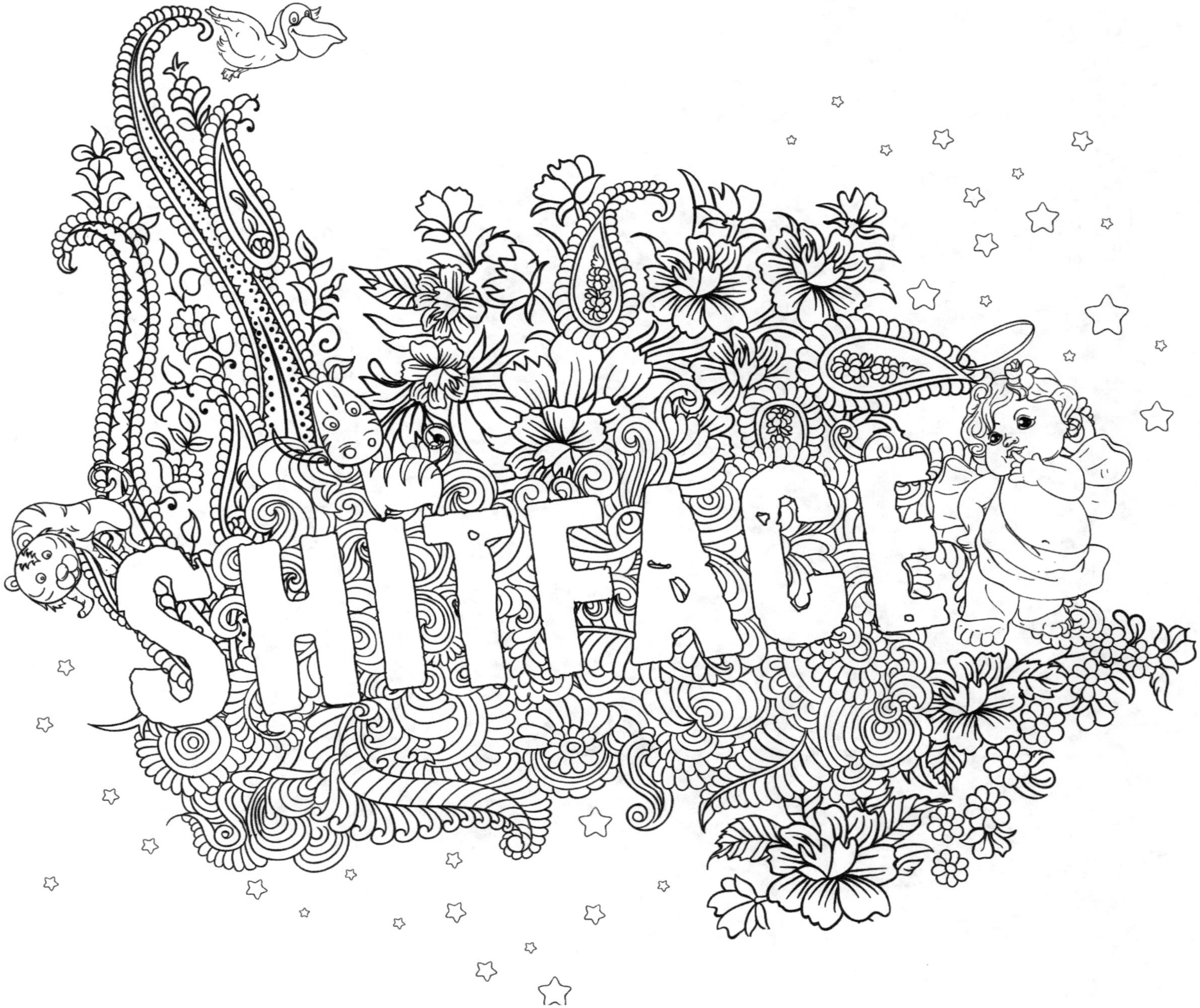
SHITFACE

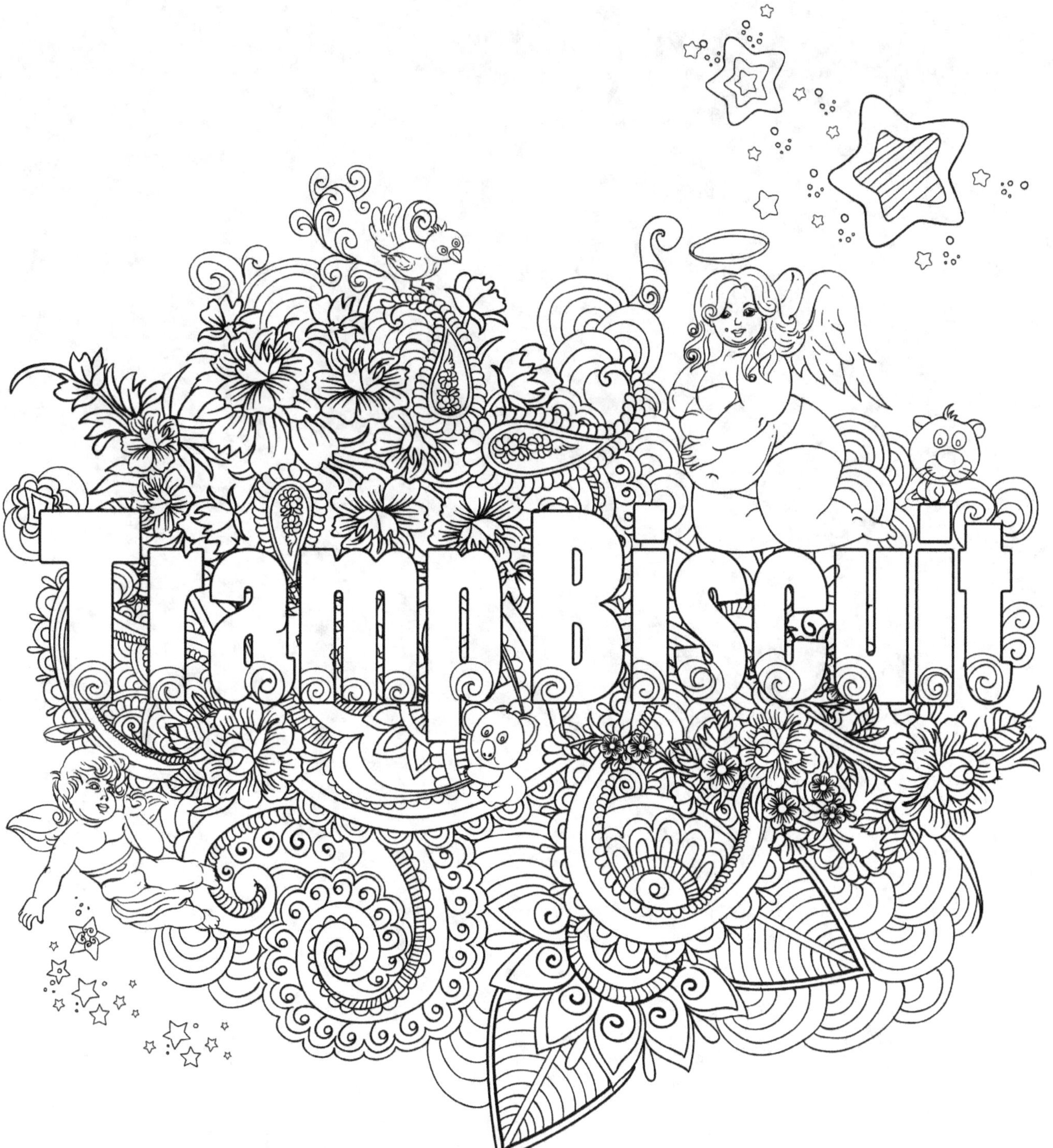
Tramp Biscuit

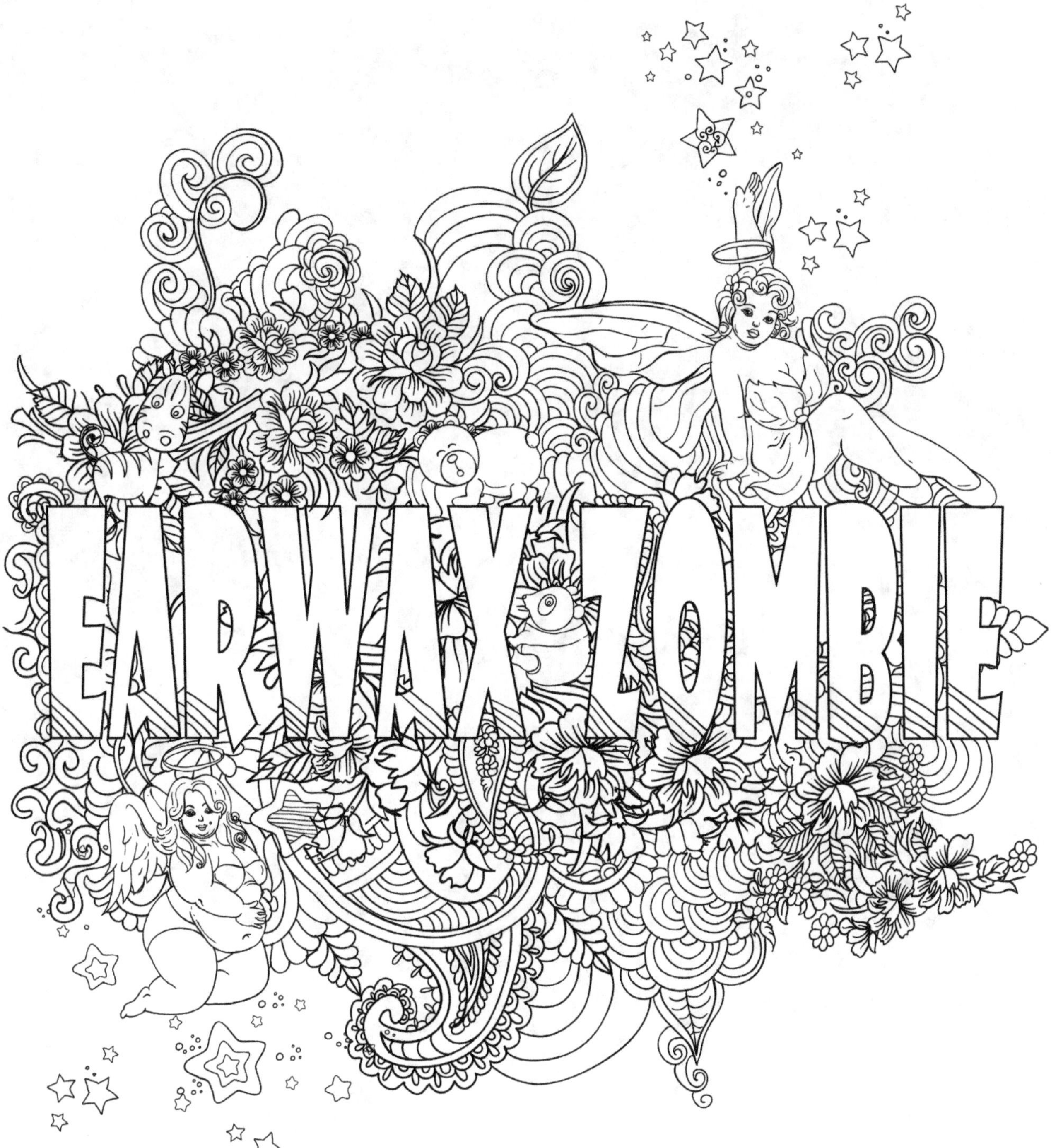
EARWAX ZOMBIE

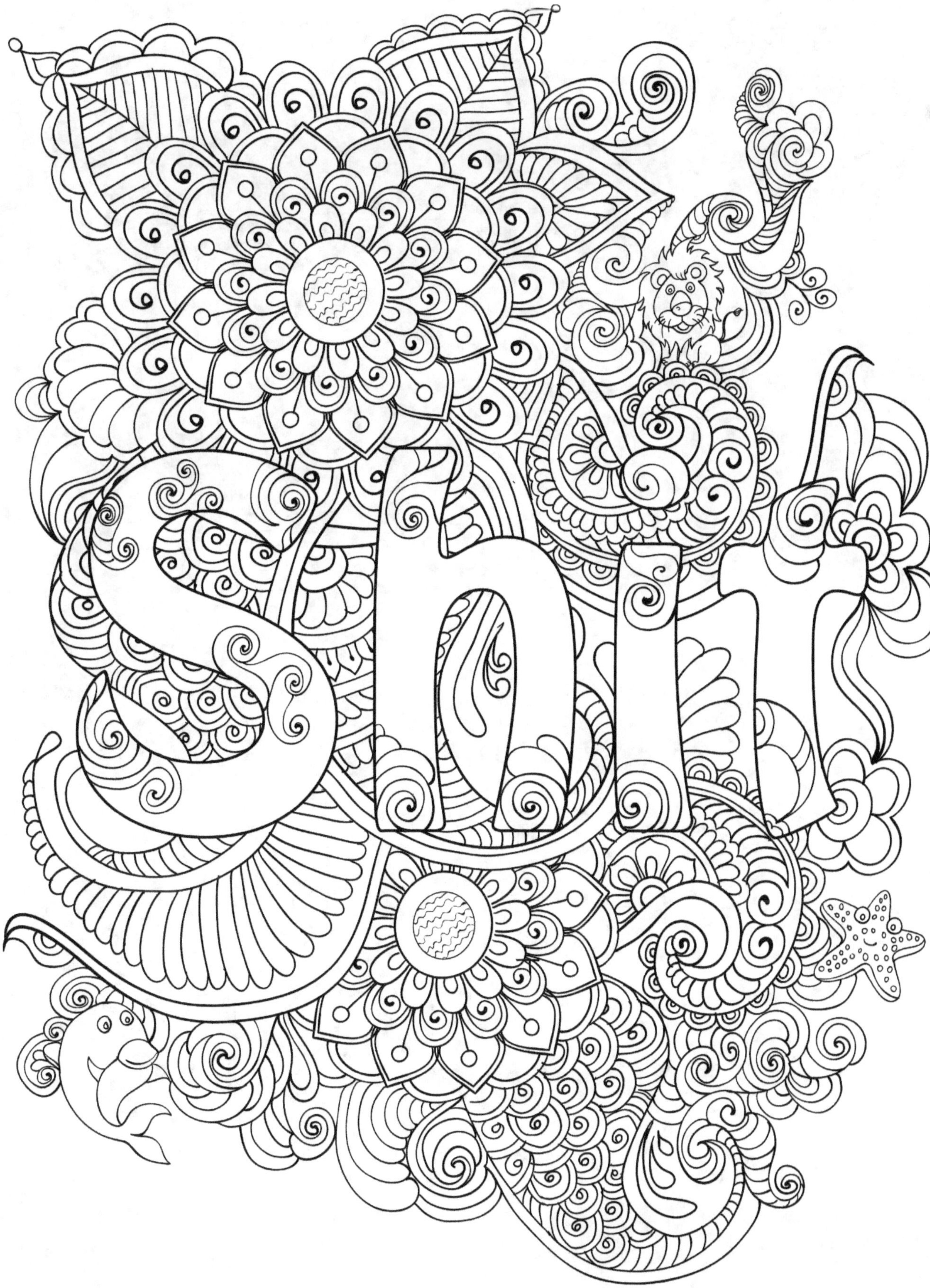
Shit

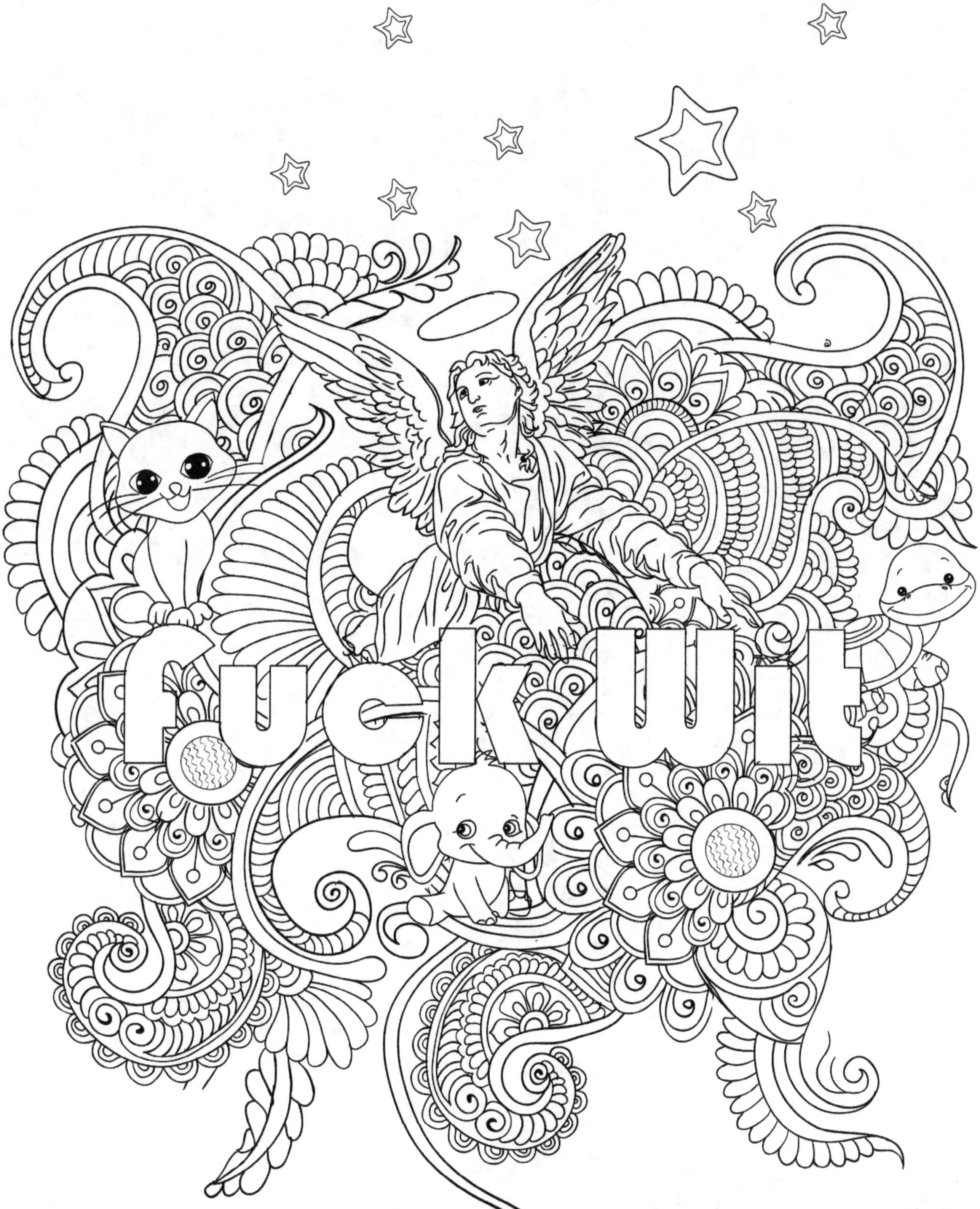
fuck wit

ISBN: 978-1523456970

Illustrated by:
Mandala & Caricature Illustration

www.ingramcontent.com/pod-product-compliance
Lightning Source LLC
Chambersburg PA
CBHW081132180526
45170CB00008B/3080